C000003085

NORTH EAST TO SOUTH WEST BY RAIL IN THE 1980S

Colin Alexander

AMBERLEY

First published 2017

Amberley Publishing
The Hill, Stroud
Gloucestershire, GL5 4EP

www.amberley-books.com

Copyright © Colin Alexander, 2017

The right of Colin Alexander to be identified
as the Author of this work has been asserted
in accordance with the Copyright, Designs and
Patents Act 1988.

ISBN 978 1 4456 6856 7 (print)
ISBN 978 1 4456 6857 4 (ebook)

All rights reserved. No part of this book may be
reprinted or reproduced or utilised in any form
or by any electronic, mechanical or other means,
now known or hereafter invented, including
photocopying and recording, or in any information
storage or retrieval system, without the permission
in writing from the Publishers.

British Library Cataloguing in Publication Data.
A catalogue record for this book is available from
the British Library.

Typesetting by Amberley Publishing.
Printed in the UK.

Introduction

Being born in Northumberland in the 1960s, and not experiencing foreign shores until I was in my twenties, meant that Cornwall, with its palm trees, was the most exotic childhood destination I knew.

My main memories of Cornish family holidays in 1973 and 1976 are of travelling behind the magnificent Class 52 Westerns. Dad had cunningly arranged our holidays in '76 to coincide with the last summer of the legendary diesel-hydraulics. My long-suffering mother was used to spending most of her holidays on or near railways.

Further back in the days when Dad and I watched the trains at Newcastle Central at the end of the 1960s, and ten years later when I was there with my mates, we paid little heed to the secondary services that travelled cross-country. Our main objects of interest were the Class 55 Deltics that were the mainstay of London–Newcastle–Edinburgh services. The arrival of the InterCity 125 High Speed Train, however, heralded a new era that saw the Deltics 'cascaded' to trains such as the Edinburgh–Plymouth.

The other event that sharpened my interest in the North East to South West route was when I started a degree course at Cornwall College in the early 1980s, which meant I became a regular passenger on the 500-mile-plus route. It was fortunate that Sony had recently introduced the revolutionary Walkman, which helped pass the time on those journeys, although I had to carry my own weight in cassettes and batteries.

My favourite quote from a train guard came during one of those journeys. Somewhere en route one of the HST power cars developed a fault, and the guard explained to us via the public address system that due to reduced speed the train would be delayed. Later, as we ground to an unscheduled halt somewhere in the middle of Devon, he added, 'The bad news is we have now lost both engines. The good news is we are not on a Boeing 737.' Genius.

That was a relatively straightforward NE–SW trip compared to one I made with my mates with a special £2 ticket in March 1981.

It went like this: Deltic No. 55007 from Newcastle to Edinburgh then No. 55002 to Leeds, where we were shunted in our coaching stock in the middle of the night by station pilot No. 08500 before No. 31317 took us to Doncaster. No. 47272 from 'Donny' to Kings Cross then No. 50015 Waterloo to Basingstoke. A replacement bus forwarded us to Micheldever for a 4-VEP to Southampton, where we caught a Southern DEMU to Salisbury. No. 50037 got us from Salisbury to Yeovil Junction then it was No. 33017 to Exeter. Disappointingly, it was No. 47487 to Plymouth, but we made up for that by taking No. 50041 back to Newton Abbot and were then double-headed by No. 50031 and No. 50049 to Plymouth. An overnight Paddington service was another pair, No. 50001 and No. 50021, which was diverted via Salisbury and Swindon. No. 55009 took us from Kings Cross to York, and the last leg was No. 47449 from York to Newcastle via Stockton. That's how we rolled.

The more conventional direct ten-hour trip from the North East coast to the western tip of England in the 1980s gave the enthusiast an opportunity to observe a variety of BR motive power, but it was also a journey of ever-changing scenery with endless interest to the casual traveller. Our journey through the pages of this book takes us from a North East dominated by Deltics, to a South West dominated by 50s, with some classes of locomotive appearing throughout the journey and some rarities popping up.

The NE–SW route was not conceived in one go; it gradually evolved piecemeal as railway mania gripped Victorian Britain, and the metals of many pre-grouping companies are used as the country is crossed diagonally.

If you are lucky enough to begin your trip in Edinburgh, the journey takes you from the great Scottish capital past Arthur's Seat and along the Firth of Forth, before transporting you over the border to Berwick. Once over the Royal Border Bridge, Northumberland's castles and coastline slip by and within an hour, Newcastle's medieval castle is passed on the approach to Central station. After the bridges of the Tyne, you pass Durham Cathedral, then the railway town of Darlington before travelling along the 'racing stretch', to enter York with its Minster and the National Railway Museum. Then it is into industrial South Yorkshire and past Chesterfield's twisted spire to the railway mecca of Derby. Power stations and motorways slip by before you burrow under the concrete of Birmingham. Subterranean New Street with its electric trains is left behind and the train plunges down the famous Lickey Incline, past Gloucester Cathedral and on towards Brunel's Bristol. The Somerset levels are left behind, bringing Devon's fearsome gradients and glorious seawalls as you are carried towards Plymouth, before moving slowly across the Royal Albert Bridge over the Tamar into beautiful Cornwall, crossing the many viaducts on this scenic route. Junction stations for charming branch lines are passed before the train slows alongside Mount's

Bay as we approach the modest terminus at Penzance. On a journey such as this, the numbers taken in a trainspotter's notebook would fill several pages.

As well as the main Edinburgh–Newcastle–Birmingham–Plymouth–Penzance route, we will briefly visit some of the other departure and terminating points of services using the NE–SW route, such as Hull, Swansea and Poole, along with the Cornish branch lines that took countless northern holidaymakers to their eventual destinations. This book relives the heady days of the 1980s, when diesels were blue and British-built.

Finally, I must thank all of the photographers who have contributed to this book, which includes some very good friends as well as many co-operative members of the wonderful Flickr community.

In the summer of 1976, my Dad took us on our second family holiday to Cornwall – by train of course. In 1973 we had used Motorail to St Austell but this time we'd left the car at home. We stayed in St Ives and used the railway for day trips to Newquay, Penzance and Plymouth, where my brother and I posed with Class 52 Western diesel-hydraulic No. D1054 *Western Governor*. It was this holiday that inspired me to apply to Cornwall College eight years later. (John Alexander MBE)

Our long journey begins in style, as English Electric Class 55 Deltic No. 55019 *Royal Highland Fusilier* gets ready to leave Waverley station with 1V93, the 09:50 Edinburgh to Plymouth service, in June 1981. The Deltic will cover the 204 miles to York and wait there to take over the return service. The clock on the North British Hotel tells us we are ten minutes from departure. (Bruce Galloway)

Celebrity Deltic No. 55002 *The King's Own Yorkshire Light Infantry*, wearing the pseudo-1960s two-tone green she received the previous year, waits for the off at Berwick-upon-Tweed in 1981 as she prepares to tackle the last 57 miles to Edinburgh with 1S27, which originated at Plymouth. The line from here to the Scottish capital belonged to the North British Railway until 1923. (Alan Hutchinson)

With part of Stephenson's Royal Border Bridge just visible above the middle of the train, we are leaving Berwick behind. The line hugs the Northumberland coast, and we will be travelling on the former North Eastern Railway for a considerable distance now. The passengers on the 07:18 Edinburgh to Carlisle service will be enjoying the North Sea views as Deltic No. 55009 *Alycidon* accelerates past Scremerston on 16 June 1981. (Pete Robins)

South West to North East trains that terminated at Newcastle would continue as empty stock to Heaton Junction for the carriage sidings there. In this scene a Class 47/4 approaches the sidings with stock for servicing in 1983. The photographer was a railway employee wearing a high-visibility vest, in case you are wondering! (David Tweddle)

In the summer months there were many extra scheduled trains to supplement the basic NE–SW timetable. No. 47255 is seen at Newcastle having arrived with one such working, 1E94, the 08:22 from Taunton on 25 August 1979. Platform 6 holds a Metro-Cammell DMU in the short-lived 'refurbished' livery. (Dave Jolly)

Occupying a similar position to No. 47255 above is that mainstay of the NE–SW route for many years, the BR Sulzer Type 4. One of the fifty Class 45/1s equipped with electric train heating (ETH) was No. 45143, which was adorned with the splendid regimental name *5th Royal Inniskilling Dragoon Guards*. (Alan Hutchinson)

Before the days of Deltics on the Edinburgh to Plymouth trains and locomotive changes at York, No. 46020 has arrived at Newcastle with 1S27, the 07:25 Plymouth to Edinburgh, on 24 February 1979. She will be uncoupled here and replaced by No. 47035, while the 46 crosses the Tyne to Gateshead for fuelling. No. 46020 was a relatively early withdrawal, being taken out of service at the end of 1980. (Dave Jolly)

The infamous Lickey Incline, south of Birmingham, will be encountered later in the book. These two Class 37s, No. 37158 and No. 37296, were employed there for the purpose of banking heavy freights up the gradient. On 11 May 1984, however, they were hastily promoted to assisting this failed HST on 1E87, the 13:28 from Paignton to Newcastle – an unusual event indeed. (Dave Jolly)

NE–SW services were not all about Devon and Cornwall. South Wales and Dorset were other destinations served by this busy trunk route. By the end of the 1980s, BR's corporate blue was giving way to a variety of new liveries. Large-logo No. 47820 is seen after arrival at Newcastle Central with the 09:00 from Poole on 2 November 1989. The blue and grey Mk 1 BG is followed by an air-conditioned Mk 2 coach in the new InterCity livery. (Kevin Lane)

No. 45114 has arrived at Newcastle with 1E04, the 07:30 from Birmingham, on 27 February 1982. Notice the two Class 03 station pilots with the Royal Mail van in between. On this day I was one of several thousand pilgrims who descended on Doncaster Works for a special open day to view the remaining Deltics, which had been withdrawn two months earlier and awaited either preservation or the cutter's torch. (Dave Jolly)

One of the Deltics on display at Doncaster that grim day was my favourite, No. 55007 *Pinza*, which is seen here at Newcastle in happier times, on 11 July 1981. She is on 1S27, the Plymouth–Edinburgh train. The east-end bay platforms are busy with Cravens and Metro-Cammell DMUs for Sunderland and Middlesbrough. (Colin Alexander)

The NE–SW route also coped with excursion traffic, such as this 'additional' from Leamington Spa, whose passengers have enjoyed rare haulage in the shape of filthy snowplough-fitted No. 37185 of Cardiff Canton depot. Note the semi-functioning roller-blind headcode panel. Newcastle Central, 9 February 1980. (Ian Charles)

Leaving Newcastle for the south, trains usually cross the Tyne on the massive King Edward VII Bridge, although Robert Stephenson's High Level Bridge of 1849 can also be used. No. 47477 is coming off the former with 1V97, the 16:06 Newcastle to Bristol Temple Meads, on 28 August 1982. Central station's arched roof can be seen to the right below the old floodlights of St James's Park. (Dave Jolly)

Lit by the setting winter sun, No. 47228 passes Gateshead depot, where a Class 40 stands with the tool vans. When passing this location, we would desperately crane our necks to see what was on shed. The Class 47 is negotiating King Edward VII Bridge Junction with 1V98, the 16:20 Newcastle to Cardiff, on 23 February 1979. (Dave Jolly)

Gateshead's No. 46011 heads an engineer's train towards Tyne Yard at Low Fell alongside the main line on 16 August 1983. The train is formed of two Clarke-Chapman self-propelled twin-jib cranes and their Gresley support coach, as well as an ex-Great Western 'Toad' brakevan. This was part of the everyday scene observed on a BR journey in the 1980s. (Malcolm Donnelly)

During the final months of the Class 55 Deltics in normal BR service, 1V93, the 09:50 Edinburgh to Plymouth, was one of the few photographable workings in the North East. On 18 July 1981, the driver of No. 55004 *Queen's Own Highlander* awaits the signal from the guard at Durham, upon which her 3,300 hp of Napier Deltic power will be unleashed at the gradient. (Andrew Donnelly)

Leaving Durham station and heading south, trains are immediately on the lofty, curved viaduct, as can be seen here on 4 September 1982. This gives passengers a superb view of the Norman cathedral and castle. No. 37038 is on a train of Mk 1s bound for Great Yarmouth as an HST approaches from the south. Many enthusiasts were headed for the East Midlands on this day as Derby works held an open day. (David Tweddle)

The most historic railway location on the route is Parkgate Junction, Darlington. At this point the Stockton & Darlington Railway of 1825 was crossed 'on the flat' by what is now the East Coast Main Line. The flat crossing is long gone but the curve to the left leads to the former S&DR route to North Road, Shildon and Bishop Auckland. A southbound HST passes on 9 January 1982. The building on the right with the ventilated roof was the Great North of England Railway engine shed, dating from 1840. (Laurie Mulrine)

Darlington Bank Top station is the location for this shot of No. 45111 *Grenadier Guardsman* on the 09:25 Weymouth to Newcastle train on 23 August 1986. Note the recently fitted high-intensity headlight between the two marker lights. No. 45111 had less than nine months left in service, although it would be another five years before scrapping took place. (Carl Looker)

No. 55004 *Queen's Own Highlander* gets away from Darlington under grey skies on 16 June 1981 with 1S27, the 07:36 Plymouth to Edinburgh. No. 55004 had the dubious honour of being the last Deltic to be cut up, which occurred at Doncaster in 1983. Fortunately, six of her sisters, along with the 1955 prototype, are preserved. (Stephen Spears)

Always eagerly anticipated on the journey was the approach to York, passing the North Yard with glimpses of freight traffic and new EMUs from the works, followed by the depot and the National Railway Museum (NRM). Examples of Classes 31, 37 and 47 await their next duties beside the NRM on 3 July 1982. A preserved steam locomotive would often be on display outside the museum. The main line passes behind the diesels. (Alan Chilestone)

A different starting point for occasional NE–SW trains was the North Yorkshire resort of Scarborough. The summer-only 10:10 Scarborough to Paignton service was unusual in that it served seaside resorts on both sides of England. No. 45140 carries the unofficial name *Mercury* as she sets off towards York, and eventually Devon, on 3 October 1987. (Ivan Stewart collection)

One of the fastest stretches on the NE–SW route is the main line from Darlington to York, where Deltic No. 55008 *The Green Howards* waits to replace No. 47482, which has just arrived from Plymouth, sometime in 1981. The Deltic will have worked south from Edinburgh and is about to return to the Scottish capital, taking most of the 44 miles to Darlington at 100 mph and above. (Alan Hutchinson)

With the sound of her twin Napier engines reverberating under the ornate and cavernous roof at York, Deltic No. 55017 *The Durham Light Infantry* draws a crowd of young admirers in June 1981. As well as collecting numbers, the platform-enders will be hoping to 'cab' the locomotive and maybe, with wallpaper and wax crayons, take a rubbing of her nameplate. (Philip Walton)

No. 45134 stands at York with the Scarborough to Paignton train on 6 June 1987, as 'the shape of things to come' lurks alongside, in the form of a West Yorkshire PTE-liveried Class 141 railbus. Thirty years on, today's passengers have to tolerate journeys in similar four-wheeled vehicles, nicknamed 'Nodding Donkeys' or 'Thatcher's Prams', among other insults. (Carl Looker)

The scene in this photo is what comes to mind if someone says to me, 'North East to South West.' The far-off halcyon days of white-cabbed Finsbury Park Deltics are recalled at York station in around 1980 as Brush Class 47 No. 47452 prepares to replace English Electric Class 55 No. 55007 *Pinza* on 1V93, the Edinburgh to Plymouth train. (Craig Oliphant)

Having been introduced on some NE–SW services in the 1980s, the HSTs didn't have it all their own way and occasionally the 'old guard' had to step in, as in this case. BR Derby-built Sulzer Peak No. 45013 has helped an ailing InterCity 125 into York with the 11:09 service from Cardiff on 25 August 1986. (Carl Looker)

Due to the tragic collapse of Penmanshiel Tunnel on 17 March 1979, in which two workers lost their lives, the Edinburgh to Plymouth train was cancelled that day. A relief train was hastily arranged to run on its timings from York. It is seen here waiting to leave York behind No. 37108 in unseasonal snow. No trains ran between Dunbar and Berwick for several months while the collapsed tunnel was replaced by a different alignment. (Lewis Bevan)

Having undoubtedly replaced a Sulzer-powered machine moments earlier, No. 55015 *Tulyar* leaves York for Edinburgh with 1S27, the 07:22 from Plymouth, on 14 February 1981. As usual, even though it is winter, the front three vestibule windows are all occupied by hardy 'bashers'. Each member of the twenty-two-strong Deltic fleet had covered a remarkable 2 million miles in service by the early 1970s. (Syd Young)

Even lowly Class 31s were employed from time to time on this busy route. Class 31/4 No. 31435 is at York awaiting departure with 1V52, the 12:55 additional train to Cardiff, on 4 April 1985. Although they did theoretically have a maximum speed of 90 mph, they would have to work hard to maintain schedule – especially the 31/4s, with the ETH drawing some of their power. (Dave Jolly)

The coaching stock of 1S27 for Edinburgh stands at York's Platform 15 as the second Napier Deltic power unit of No. 55016 *Gordon Highlander* erupts into life in readiness to replace the locomotive that has arrived from Plymouth. The Deltics' career on BR spanned almost twenty-one years, being introduced in early 1961 and the last being withdrawn at the beginning of 1982. (Ian Beattie)

On 20 June 1981, Brush Type 4 Class 47/4 No. 47533 has arrived at York's Platform 15 with 1S27, the 07:36 Plymouth to Edinburgh, and is about to be replaced by Class 55 No. 55011 *The Royal Northumberland Fusiliers*. By this time the remaining Deltics were all concentrated at York depot; all would be withdrawn in a little over six months. (Dave Jolly)

It was not unusual to see Class 50s taking 1V93 from York to Plymouth as a means of returning to the Western Region (WR) after overhaul at Doncaster. It was, however, rare to see a Class 50 arriving *from* the WR, as in the case of No. 50026 *Indomitable*, which has reached York on the 09:06 additional train from Bristol Temple Meads on 2 April 1985. (Carl Looker)

A year later and No. 50026 *Indomitable* is back at York, this time awaiting departure with 1V85, the 09:22 Newcastle to Penzance train. As was the custom, this working is to return her to Plymouth's Laira depot following her visit to Doncaster works. The date is 11 April 1986, by which time InterCity livery was beginning to appear on coaching stock. (Dave Jolly)

South of York, NE–SW trains could be routed either via Doncaster, Leeds or the direct route to Sheffield. Taking the Leeds line at Church Fenton is No. 47658 on 1V65, the 09:43 Newcastle to Penzance on 16 December 1986. At about this time I bade farewell to life in Cornwall, as a semester at Louisiana State University followed by eight years working in London was about to begin. (Carl Looker)

Leeds' soulless 1960s city station was an alternative North East starting point for some South Western services. No. 47552, however, is already 105 miles into her journey as she waits for departure with 1V65, the 09:43 Newcastle to Penzance, on 8 November 1986. In order to cure reliability issues early in their lives, the Class 47's Sulzer power units had been de-rated from 2,750 to 2,580 hp. (Dave Jolly)

The east coast port of Kingston-upon-Hull was another location that boasted a South West destination. No. 47406 was one of the original batch of twenty Brush Type 4s, known as 'generators'. She is wearing InterCity livery and carrying 'Rail Riders' nameplates, after the BR's kids' club of the time, as she waits at Hull Paragon at the head of the 10:54 to Cardiff on 15 December 1985. (Carl Looker)

The last ever working of the return train 1E79, the 13:55 Cardiff to Hull, was on 10 May 1986, and a few enthusiasts turned out to mark the occasion. Here it is at Doncaster behind Western Region No. 47623, formerly No. 47090, and still carrying her *Vulcan* nameplates. The building on the right is part of the once-vast Doncaster Works. (Carl Looker)

At Normanton we leave the former North Eastern Railway for ex-Midland metals. Gateshead's No. 46038 is passing with 'Cobra' container empties from Wakefield to Derwenthaugh on 26 February 1982. Still in place is the old station footbridge to the island platform and two BR mess vans are parked up for the playing of cards and the reading of newspapers. (Chris Davis)

The floodlights of Rotherham United's old Millmoor ground form the backdrop as a Class 45/1 heads for Sheffield and the South West on 21 April 1979. On this day, I passed this location on a memorable railtour from Newcastle behind LNER V2 No. 4771 *Green Arrow*. She took us via the Hope Valley to Dinting where EM1 electrics Nos 76014 and 76030 hauled us through Woodhead to Tinsley. LNER K1 No. 2005 and Deltic No. 55022 were also involved. (Paul Braybrook)

Brightside is the ironically named station to the north of Sheffield, where immaculate No. 50001 *Dreadnought* adds a welcome splash of colour as she returns to the Western Region following a Doncaster overhaul in 1980. The English Electric Class 50s were the only BR diesel locomotives apart from the Deltics that were permitted to run at 100 mph. (Paul Braybrook)

I always liked Sheffield Midland station, which was 46 miles from York and usually home to some interesting locomotives. One thing I never saw there though was a Class 58. Almost-new 3,300 hp Railfreight No. 58014 has arrived at Sheffield with 'The South Yorkshireman' railtour on 15 July 1984 – two months before I started college in Cornwall. (Ian Beattie)

No. 37013 stands at Sheffield's Platform 2 with a SW–NE train as a Swindon-built Class 124 departs from Platform 1 with a Hull service. These 'Trans-Pennine' DMUs were powerful and stylish, and were introduced in 1960 on the Hull to Liverpool route as six-car sets, which included a buffet-car. By July 1983 when this photo was taken, they had lost their catering facilities long ago and were relegated to secondary duties, to be withdrawn the following year. (Paul Braybrook)

One of the less well-known summer services originated at Tenby in the far south-west of Wales and terminated at York. On 1 July 1989, the 3,500 hp English Electric combination of metals sector No. 37110 and large-logo No. 37203 leaves Sheffield Midland with 1E33, the 08:20 Tenby to York train. I wonder what the ratio is of returning holidaymakers versus Class 37 'bashers'? (Dave Jolly)

More typical of SW–NE motive power is No. 47140, which ticks over at Sheffield Midland having arrived with 1E18, the 16:08 Bristol Temple Meads to Newcastle, on 30 May 1981. Note the sacks of mail being loaded or unloaded and the ancient barrow in use. These were a feature of most major stations and doubled as seats for railway enthusiasts. (Dave Jolly)

'Split head-code' Class 45 No. 45027 stands at Sheffield with the 14:37 Leeds to Plymouth train on 16 May 1981. On this day my mates and I passed through here en route to the Severn Valley Railway on a BR 'Merrymaker' excursion. This featured No. 45013 from Newcastle to Birmingham, and Nos 25056 and 25130 thereafter to Bewdley. Sadly, there is no room on the modern railway for the Merrymaker. (Dave Jolly)

5 October 1981 was an auspicious occasion at Sheffield as it witnessed its first High Speed Train (HST) service. One of the twin 2,250 hp Paxman-engined power-cars, No. 43166, leads the formation into Platform 1 with 1E10, the inaugural Swansea to Leeds InterCity 125. (Paul Braybrook)

English Electric 1,750 hp Class 37 No. 37058 would be of far more interest to the discerning enthusiast of the 1980s than any HST. Sheffield Midland's Platform 6 is occupied by 1V32, the 10:32 York to Penzance additional train on 17 August 1985. One of the most versatile types of BR diesel loco, many 37s are still in service today – the first being introduced in 1960. (Dave Jolly)

The Class 37's larger, 2,000 hp sister, the English Electric Class 40, was not a regular sight in the South West, but were common on the route north of Birmingham. No. 40086 has just arrived at Sheffield on 26 June 1984 with the morning parcels service from Doncaster. On the right, No. 47473 waits to leave with a service to Birmingham New Street. (Syd Young)

Type 2 diesels stand side by side at Sheffield Midland as BR Sulzer 1,250 hp Class 25 No. 25211 waits with the 14:25 York to Plymouth additional service on 28 May 1985. A Brush Class 31/4 stands alongside. All 263 Class 31 locomotives were re-equipped in the 1960s, with 1,470 hp English Electric power units replacing the original Mirrlees engines. (Carl Looker)

Summer weekend additional trains often meant unusual traction as locos usually reserved for weekday freight workings were pressed into service. Pairs of 1,000 hp English Electric Class 20s were employed on Skegness trains, but it was extremely rare for a single 20 to appear on a main line service like this. Sheffield sees No. 20011, one of the original 1957 'Pilot Scheme' locomotives, on the 12:55 York to Birmingham 'extra' on 27 August 1985. (Carl Looker)

By the mid-1980s, the HST fleet had not only taken over the East Coast and Western Region main lines, but were also diagrammed on many NE–SW services. No. W43033 is seen in its new InterCity livery at Sheffield Midland with a Plymouth service on 5 February 1988. A Metro-Cammell DMU passes through the centre road. (Syd Young)

A pleasing Sheffield nocturne is brought to life by the steam-heating boiler of No. 45077 as she heads a Bristol Temple Meads to Leeds City additional train on 15 February 1985. Train-heating boilers were often the Achilles heel of diesel loco reliability, and by the 1980s electric train heating (ETH) was taking over. The Class 45/1 sub-class were fitted for ETH working. (Carl Looker)

Chesterfield station was usually the next stop after Sheffield. No. 31293 has called there with 1Z45, the 13:48 York to Newton Abbot additional train, on 25 May 1987. Due to engineering work near Sheffield at the time, this train and several others ran direct from Rotherham to Chesterfield via 'The Old Road'. (Dave Jolly)

English Electric to the rescue as Nos 20146 and 20031 depart Chesterfield. Class 45 No. 45058 had failed there on the 15:54 York to Bristol Temple Meads, a service that was booked for an HST. The date is 15 August 1986 and, at that time, rescue locomotives were never far away, unlike the modern, rationalised railway. (Carl Looker)

One of the landmarks we always looked out for on the route was the twisted wooden spire of Chesterfield's parish church of St Mary and All Saints. It can be seen in the background of this atmospheric photo of No. 46032 heading north with 'Sealion' ballast hoppers on a gloomy 28 February 1983. This 46 was one of the last sixteen to make it into 1984, before it was withdrawn that April. (Kev Smith)

Of the many locations passed en route from NE to SW, one of the most exciting from an enthusiast's point of view was Derby, home to the BREL Works and the Railway Technical Centre (RTC). On 26 May 1988, RTC departmental locomotives No. 97403 (ex-No. 46035), No. 97201 (No. 24061) and No. 97204 (No. 31326) were captured from a passing train outside Derby Etches Park. (Syd Young)

Typical of the sights seen from the train on the NE–SW route is BR Sulzer Class 25 No. 25135, which is seen with a parcels train at Derby in the early 1980s. In my experience, such a train would pass between me and an engine shed packed with locomotives just as my train passed, completely blocking my view. (Ian Beattie)

A rake of Network SouthEast's colourful coaches forms 1V57, the 14:33 York to Taunton, as it coasts into Derby on 2 July 1988. One gets the impression that a fair percentage of the passengers are 'Peak Bashers'! No. 45046, her *Royal Fusilier* nameplates replaced by painted versions, has exactly one month left in service, becoming the last Class 45/0 to be withdrawn, which occurred on 2 August. (Dave Jolly)

It was always a treat when something other than the usual Sulzer Type 4 turned up. Complete with a steam-style Tinsley shed code plate on her nose, No. 37228 arrives at Derby on 4 September 1982 with 1V22, the 08:23 York to Tenby. It is likely that most of the passengers will be heading for the annual Derby Works open day. (Syd Young)

Class 47/4 No. 47435 starts away from Derby with 1E63, the 09:55 Weymouth to Newcastle train, on 4 July 1987. Numbered D1550 when new, she spent her career on the Eastern, North Eastern and Scottish regions of BR, and would be withdrawn in 1990 after a twenty-six-year career – a relatively short lifespan for a 47. (Dave Jolly)

Burton-on-Trent station was surrounded by the brewery industry, and there was always freight traffic on view as well as locos to look out for at the stabling point. On 2 July 1979, Nos 20159 and 20157 haul No. 56054 southbound through the station. I had seen No. 56054 nearing completion in Doncaster Works the previous year and, in 1983, No. 20159 was one of a pair of 20s that took me from Skegness to Nottingham. (Andrew Walker)

As Tamworth (High Level) was reached, with luck we would catch a glimpse of an electric train on the West Coast Main Line, which crossed below the NE–SW route almost at right angles. Class 47 No. 47616 *Y Ddraig Goch* (The Red Dragon) is the appropriately named loco in charge of the 07.17 Derby to Cardiff on a wet 16 April 1986. (Lewis Bevan)

Saltley Depot was passed on the approach to Birmingham, but the view from the main line was brief and frustrating. This typical mid-1980s scene at the shed includes two members of Class 25 and a pair of 31s flanked by a 56 and a named 47. It also shows how difficult it was to record loco numbers from a moving train! (Rob Walton)

The main crossroads encountered on the NE–SW route was Birmingham New Street, where trains arrived and departed in all directions. On 24 April 1982, No. 50014 *Warspite* emerges from the stygian gloom at the west end of the station to take over a train to the South West. I was working my way from Newcastle to Plymouth for Laira Depot open day. (Colin Alexander)

On the NE–SW route at Birmingham we enjoyed a second encounter with electrified West Coast Main Line services. A member of Class 81, formerly AL1, No. 81012 stands between duties at New Street on 9 July 1983. The 81s were one of five classes making up the first hundred AC electric locos. The class of twenty-five was built by BRCW at nearby Smethwick. (Paul James)

No. 47447 stands at a wintry Birmingham New Street after arrival with 1O09, the 08:12 Newcastle to Poole train, on 17 January 1987. In the four-character train-describer code, the first number '1' represents an express passenger train, the letter 'O' means the destination is the Southern Region, and the last two digits identify the train. The Western Region was 'V', and the Eastern and Scottish were 'E' and 'S' respectively. (Dave Jolly)

Another change from all the Type 4 traction is this pair of 37s, with No. 37002 leading No. 37192 at Birmingham New Street on 7 July 1984 with the 09:30 Poole to Newcastle additional service. Those were the days when BR had spare coaching stock and locomotives and could put into service extra trains to cope with demand. (Lewis Bevan)

Summer sunshine on the large-logo livery of No. 50023 *Howe* adds a welcome splash of colour at Birmingham New Street, where she has arrived with a Bristol to Edinburgh train on 15 June 1985. Something else of interest seems to have caught the attention of the spotters on the platform. Five days after this photo was taken, I was on my way to my first Glastonbury Festival. (Lewis Bevan)

The early 1980s was an interesting time to be a railway enthusiast. Birmingham New Street was a busy hub with a wide variety of classes on show. The pride of the West Coast Main Line's fleet were the Class 87 electrics, and one of these, No. 87032 *Kenilworth*, waits for the 'off' with a Down express. (Ian Robinson)

On 2 July 1988, No. 45107 stands at Birmingham New Street working a Leeds to Poole train. The former D43 was withdrawn from service only days after this photo was taken. The long reign of the Peaks on the NE–SW was coming to a close, with the last of the Class being taken out of service in February 1989. A Class 85 electric locomotive waits alongside. (Lewis Bevan)

In this New Street scene, No. 50004 *St Vincent* is preparing to work to Paddington and unique thyristor-control No. 87101 *Stephenson* is bound for Euston. The photo, taken 26 May 1988, conveys the variety that could be seen at New Street in those days. From Birmingham, trains from the North East headed either for Poole, Bristol or Cardiff. (Syd Young)

The first time I travelled the NE–SW route beyond Sheffield without my parents was on 28 June 1980. No. 46025 hauled us from Newcastle to Birmingham on the 'Severn Valley Invader', where Nos 25305 and 25308 took over. The Type 2s ran via Kidderminster to Bewdley, where they awaited uncoupling, and the ex-GWR combination of 0-6-0 No. 3205 and 4-6-0 No. 7812 *Erlestoke Manor* took us the rest of the way to Bridgnorth. (Ian Beattie)

Trains bound for Poole or Weymouth took the former Great Western Railway line from Birmingham through Banbury and Oxford to Reading. No. 50046 *Ajax* stands in the summer sunshine at Oxford with a southbound train in July 1980. We were on a family holiday at a farm in Wiltshire at the time, but I escaped with my camera to the railway most days. (Colin Alexander)

Network SouthEast-liveried No. 50028 *Tiger* was captured at Reading on the 12:03 Poole to Newcastle train on 1 April 1989. Having arrived here via Southampton and Basingstoke, the train reversed before continuing on GWR metals to Birmingham. The locomotive is just about to be uncoupled by the orange-clad shunter, who waits to duck under the buffers. (Carl Looker)

Unusual traction for the Poole to Newcastle train one day in 1983. The Southern Region's No. 33114 stands at Basingstoke. The nineteen locomotives in the Class 33/1 subclass were fitted for push-pull working and could be seen propelling 4TC unpowered units, which were driven remotely from the cab at the front of the train. (Brian McCulloch)

Passengers on trains like the Newcastle to Poole service would be able to observe Southern Region third-rail electrics, such as these two at Worting Junction, just west of Basingstoke, on 16 September 1985. On the left is 4-VEP No. 7748 on the Southampton line and heading east towards Basingstoke is 2-HAP No. 6080 with 4-VEP No. 7719 behind it. (Paul James)

Poole-bound passengers could enjoy a sight like this as Eastleigh was reached. This was the view from Bishopstoke Road Bridge on 8 August 1986 with No. 56032 *Merehead* passing the station next to No. 59002, which was then only months old. The EMD-built 59s were the first post-war American locos in Britain and were the ancestors of today's ubiquitous Class 66s. Also in the shot are No. 33107, No. 33011, No. 47242, electro-diesel No. 73135 and No. 47157. (David Hann)

Southampton was the next major stop on the Newcastle to Poole route. 10 June 1983 was the first day of an All-Line Railrover and we'd travelled overnight from Newcastle to London. Our first daylight move was electro-diesel No. 73129 from Waterloo to Southampton, and then a Southern Region English Electric-powered DEMU took us to Fareham. From there we got narrow-bodied No. 33204 back to Southampton, as seen here. (Colin Alexander)

Bristol Bath Road's No. 47557 is framed by Bournemouth's overall roof as she waits for departure time with 1E63, the 10.40 Poole to Newcastle, on 26 March 1988. She was later renumbered No. 47721 *Saint Bede*, and as such lasted in service until 2002, being scrapped by EMR at Kingsbury in May 2007. (Mark Few)

From Basingstoke to Poole, the route was that of the erstwhile London & South Western Railway. With a semaphore home signal dominating the foreground, No. 47439 passes Poole signal box as she approaches the station with the empty stock to form the 17:05 to Derby on 16 September 1982. (Lewis Bevan)

After our Dorset detour it's back to the NE–SW route south of Birmingham. Blackwell is the summit of the notorious Lickey Incline, where northbound trains contend with a gradient of 1 in 37. In steam days bankers were essential but No. 50029 *Renown* is unassisted on the 08:17 Penzance to Edinburgh/Glasgow on 27 August 1988. An AC electric loco would take over at Birmingham and at Carstairs the train would divide for the two Scottish cities. (Carl Looker)

No. 37171 is on the 2-mile ascent of the Lickey on 1 April 1986 with 6E58, the 16:15 Bromsgrove to Lindsey Refinery. A total of 309 of these highly successful English Electric Type 3s were built from 1960 by Vulcan Foundry and Robert Stephenson & Hawthorns, and this is one of several that is still in service in 2017, now numbered No. 37611 in the DRS fleet. (Ian Holmes)

Class 40s were relatively rare south-west of Birmingham but No. 40024, formerly named *Lucania*, is at the foot of the Lickey Incline on 28 April 1984. She is passing 'bankers' No. 37295 and No. 37129 as she heads 1Z39, the Severn Valley Railway's 'South Wales Whistler' – a Leeds to Carmarthen charter. (Don Gatehouse)

No. 50038 *Formidable* has arrived at Cheltenham Spa with 1M78, the 13:10 Plymouth to Manchester Piccadilly, on 7 July 1985. About half an hour after departure she will reach Bromsgrove where the assault on the Lickey begins. South of Cheltenham, trains can enter Gloucester station in the Cardiff direction, or continue to Bristol. (Dave Jolly)

Gloucester's former Great Western Railway station has Britain's second longest platform, which is beaten only by that at Colchester. Most NE–SW services bypassed Gloucester but those that called here, such as the 08:45 Aberdeen and Glasgow to Plymouth, would have to reverse. This is No. 50045 *Achilles* and the date is 23 September 1988. (Carl Looker)

Before we venture further into the South West of England, we will continue beyond Gloucester on the ex-GWR line into South Wales. This hugs the north bank of the Severn before crossing the River Wye at Chepstow, where No. 45115 is passing on a Cardiff-bound train on 4 November 1982. A total of 127 Class 45s were built, as well as fifty-six of the Class 46 variants. (Adrian Nicholls)

At Severn Tunnel Junction, Cardiff-bound trains from the North East must take their turn with those from London as the latter emerge from Britain's longest main line tunnel. Plenty of locos could be observed here from passing trains. No. 25190 had just arrived light engine from the west on 7 May 1986 and was headed for the stabling point, along with No. 47298. One of South Wales' many Class 37s is visible on the other side of the main line. (John Dedman)

No. 37230 passes Newport with a freight working on 10 March 1989 as a local DMU stands at Platform 2. The spacious station was opened in 1850, being extended in 1928 and again in 2007 in readiness for the 2010 Ryder Cup at nearby Celtic Manor. No. 37230 was withdrawn in 2005 after a forty-one-year career. (Roddy MacPhee)

Another depot we would speed past, frantically scribbling down perhaps a third of the loco numbers, was Ebbw Junction, just west of Newport. On 13 April 1980 there were a number of Class 37s on view, along with some departmental coaches and a snowplough. In the centre of the picture is No. 56045, behind which a Class 08 shunter can be glimpsed. (Paul James)

At Cardiff Central on 23 July 1987, No. 37692 passes slowly by with the General Manager's saloon. Delivered in 1963 as No. D6822 from Robert Stephenson & Hawthorn's, the loco would be renumbered No. 37122 in the 1970s. She was re-geared as a dedicated freight loco and became No. 37692 in 1986. She was withdrawn in 2004 and cut up by C. F. Booth in Rotherham in 2009. (Terry Callaghan)

Cardiff Canton shed was reasonably accessible on foot, but if passing on a train the usual difficulties applied if trying to record numbers. In this shot taken on 6 February 1988, three EE Class 37s, one of which has had a serious nose job, are joined by a Class 56. All are wearing the kind of livery variations that brightened up the rail scene in the late 1980s. (Terry Callaghan)

This fine study give us a rare glimpse inside the carriage sheds at Cardiff Canton as No. 50005 *Collingwood* collects empty stock. She is in the company of a mixture of 'Heritage' DMUs and some of the then-new 'Sprinters', which began to enter service in the mid-1980s – both of which would be used on South Wales valley lines. (Ian Charles)

A silver-roofed Class 47 slows for the approach to Swansea, passing the sidings at Landore with a train that includes two postal vans. This was 20 March 1982, and the previous night No. 3122 had brought us from Newcastle on the overnight Bristol train, 1V50, via Worcester and Gloucester – a journey of over 298 miles. We returned from Swansea to Tyneside via Crewe and Sleaford, naturally. (Colin Alexander)

No. 50018 *Resolution* is carrying the colourful livery of Network SouthEast as she awaits departure from Swansea with a newspaper train for Old Oak Common in the mid-1980s. The Class 50s had suffered from reliability issues in their early days, partly due to problems with the various electronic systems installed. However, they gave good service following refurbishment at Doncaster in the late 1970s and early '80s. (Steve Powell)

Celebrity green-liveried No. 47484 *Isambard Kingdom Brunel* has arrived at Swansea with a much shorter parcels train. Until BR began naming large numbers of the class in the early 1980s, No. 47484 was one of only seventeen Brush Type 4s to carry names, all of which were Western Region examples. On today's railway there are no through trains from Newcastle to South Wales. (Steve Powell)

Retracing our route back up the Severn we re-join the main line at Stoke Gifford yard, the site of Bristol Parkway station. The NE–SW route has left the former Midland Railway and we are now on Great Western metals. Far from home, No. 37039 of Glasgow's Eastfield shed brings a heavy Weston-super-Mare to York service through Parkway on 15 July 1984. She survives in service at the time of writing as DRS No. 37603. ('Mangotsfield Mike')

Beneath the graceful train shed in a deserted Bristol Temple Meads station stands No. 50046 *Ajax* on 1F84, on 7 October 1987. This beautiful nocturnal scene is enhanced by reflections on the wet platform. We spent many a night on overnight trains in our youth – yet another aspect of railway operation that is virtually no more. (Douglas Johnson)

The railway took on a different character at night with newspaper and parcels trains vying for paths and platforms with overnight passenger and sleeper trains. Up and down the country, postal workers would be loading, unloading and sorting mail from trains. No. 45124 is carrying the unofficial painted name *Unicorn* as she stands at Bristol with two GUV parcels vans on 7 October 1987. (Douglas Johnson)

The instantly recognisable southern approach to Bristol Temple Meads on 24 April 1982, as No. 50018 *Resolution* arrives from the Exeter direction. No. 46009 had brought me here from Newcastle, and I would continue my journey to Plymouth behind No. 50022 *Anson*. I was headed for the open day at Laira Depot. (Colin Alexander)

No. 47500, appropriately named *Great Western*, arrives at Bristol from the South West on 28 April 1984 on a train of Mk 1 coaching stock. The following year No. 47500 was painted in GWR green as part of the 150th anniversary celebrations. No. 56045 can be seen at Bath Road Depot on the left. The 3,250 hp Class 56s were built for heavy freight duties from 1977 in Romania, Doncaster and Crewe. (Syd Young)

On 12 September 1978, No. 45041 *Royal Tank Regiment* arrives at Bristol from the South West with an inter-regional train, whose formation includes 'High Speed Track Recording Coach' No. RDB 999550. Perhaps this was bound for Derby's Railway Technical Centre? By way of contrast, a steam crane can be seen at Bath Road shed to the left. (Syd Young)

Apart from Class 50s, the other diesel type not usually found in the North East in the 1980s, but regularly seen in the South West, was the Southern Region's Class 33. One of ninety-eight built, No. 33008 negotiates the curve at the north end of Bristol Temple Meads as she arrives in April 1982, either from Portsmouth or Cardiff. (Colin Alexander)

Twin Peaks at Bristol Temple Meads. It is 2 June 1979 and, nine months after the top photo on p. 57, No. 45041 *Royal Tank Regiment* has lost her original black headcode panels in favour of marker lights. She is on the 08:28 Paignton to Sheffield (left) and next to her is Gateshead's No. 46052 on the 10:18 Weston-super-Mare to Birmingham New Street. (Lewis Bevan)

Temple Meads was a rarity among BR stations in that it gave spotters a good vantage point to observe the comings and goings of a major locomotive depot at close hand. No. 50015 *Valiant* is at Bristol Bath Road shed on 29 March 1982. Like many of her sisters, she is now preserved, and is a regular performer at the East Lancashire Railway. (Stephen Dance)

In the bright sunshine of 15 June 1985, a very clean No. 45126 departs Bristol with 1V64, the 07:17 Derby to Penzance. The 45s and 46s, which were synonymous with the NE–SW route, were powered by Sulzer 2,500 hp power units. They were developed from the earlier 44s, which were named after British mountains, hence the generic nickname 'Peak' for all three classes. (Dave Jolly)

Unrefurbished No. 50034 *Furious* is in charge of a train for Plymouth at Bristol Temple Meads on 10 April 1980. Alongside is No. 47157 and another 47 lurks to the right of shot. On this particular day I was hundreds of miles away, travelling on Deltics No. 55002 and No. 55016 between Berwick and Darlington. (Lewis Bevan)

The sole named Class 46, No. 46026 *Leicestershire* and *Derbyshire Yeomanry,* is departing Bristol with 1V41, a York to Plymouth service, on 28 April 1984. She was withdrawn in November that year. While Syd was photographing blue diesels at Bristol, on this very day I was on the North Yorkshire Moors Railway enjoying haulage behind Nos D9529, D8568, D7029, D821 and 55019. (Syd Young)

The 1,550 hp Sulzer-powered Class 33s, built by Birmingham Railway Carriage & Wagon Co., were a commonplace sight around Bristol in the 1980s. No. 33009 stands at Temple Meads in 1984, probably having arrived from Portsmouth. (Colin Alexander)

A Class 45 undergoes a crew change in this atmospheric portrait at Bristol Temple Meads in about 1980 as she breaks her journey from North East to South West. Excess steam issues from her train-heating boiler. From here we follow the route of the former broad-gauge Bristol & Exeter Railway, which was later absorbed by the GWR. (Ian Charles)

On a loop off the main line is Weston-super-Mare, which is seen from Drove Road Bridge on 15 April 1986. The old gasworks sidings on the left follow the alignment of the original 1841 branch. In the platforms, a Class 33 and an HST both wait to depart for Bristol. Above the HST power car is the long-redundant Bristol & Exeter Railway signal box of 1866. To the right are the carriage sidings that used to be Locking Road excursion station, which closed in 1964. (Kevin Redwood)

Many ex-BR diesel locos could be seen in industrial use at the time and one to look out for en route from NE to SW was at Bridgwater, where the local cellophane works employed former Class 03 204 hp diesel-mechanical shunter No. D2133, as pictured here in 1991. Happily, this loco is now preserved at the West Somerset Railway. (Richard Vogel)

Southbound trains from the North East cross the Western Region main line from Paddington on the flyover, seen just above the rear coach, at Cogload Junction to the east of Taunton. Northbound services such as this one, hauled by No. 50026 *Indomitable* on 15 July 1984, have the easier task of following the curve as they head for Bristol. (Frank Struben)

Looking east at Cogload Junction on 26 June 1982, pioneer Class 50 No. 50050 *Fearless*, formerly No. D400, speeds by on a lightly loaded Paddington to St Austell motorail train. To the right of the semaphore signals in the distance, the flyover carrying the southbound NE–SW route over the WR main line can be seen once again. (David Payne)

Like Nos 47484 and 47500, No. 50007 *Hercules* was repainted for the 150th anniversary of the GWR, being renamed *Sir Edward Elgar* at the same time. Here she is passing an array of ground signals at Taunton in June 1984. I had travelled through here the previous month for my college interview, and would be back in September to start my course in Cornwall. (Edwin Walton)

Passing under a fine gantry of ex-GWR lower-quadrant semaphore signals, No. 50048 *Dauntless* leaves Taunton for the west in the mid-1980s. A Class 31 is parked in the sidings on the site of the former engine shed. The curve to the right once looped past the goods shed and back to re-join the main line to the east of the station. (Edwin Walton)

Unique to the Western Region was its class of five departmental Ruston & Hornsby 165 hp diesel-electric shunters allocated to the permanent way department. I often saw Taunton-based No. PWM652 when passing through Somerset. By the time this photo was taken her blue livery has been replaced by yellow and she is renumbered 97652. (Simon Close)

West of Taunton the line takes on an entirely different character as it tunnels and weaves its way through the rolling countryside of West Somerset and westward into Devon. No. 50022 *Anson* has just emerged from Whiteball Tunnel with the 09:15 Paddington to Penzance train on 25 June 1983. (Stephen Dance)

A Class 47/4 heads west past Tiverton Junction station in June 1984. Previously named Tiverton Road, it had long ceased to be a junction, and two years later the station closed completely, to be replaced by the new Tiverton Parkway (even further from the town of Tiverton, which is seven miles distant). (Edwin Walton)

No. 45121 was adorned with a white lower bodyside stripe and red buffer beams by her home depot of Toton. She is arriving at Exeter St Davids on 13 June 1981 with 1V83, the 08:05 Newcastle to Newquay train. Note the crossing attendant present to prevent pedestrians entering, as the wicket gates were not interlocked with the crossing. (Paul Robertson collection)

The platform-enders are out in force at Exeter St Davids on 13 June 1981. A Class 47 is on a train for the west as No. 33050 and No. 33065 get ready to depart with the double-headed 13:40 to Brighton. They will no doubt make a spirited departure as they climb the steeply graded curve up to Exeter Central. (Kevin Weston)

A locomotive that was always associated with the Western Region, green-liveried No. 47484 *Isambard Kingdom Brunel* arrives at Exeter St Davids on the 09:58 Penzance to Leeds on 4 July 1987. The former London & South Western Railway route to Exeter Central, Salisbury and Waterloo curves uphill to the left. (Lewis Bevan)

This was the scene at the stabling point alongside Exeter St Davids station on 24 June 1988. The driver of No. 50042 *Triumph* has collected his instructions from the signal box and is about to bring his charge off the shed. In the background, No. 31119 is stabled along with an unknown Class 08 shunter. (Dave Gommersall)

Large-logo liveried No. 47450 is at Exeter St Davids on 24 June 1989 with 1M07, the 08:37 Plymouth to Liverpool Lime Street train. The 47 would work to Birmingham, where it would be replaced by an electric loco for the journey to Merseyside. 512 Brush Type 4s were built, later to become Class 47s, and many are still in service now, with some having been re-engined with EMD power units as Class 57s. (Roddy MacPhee)

A regular traffic flow on the route from Cornwall to the Midlands was china clay for the Potteries. No. 45032 pauses on the centre road at Exeter St Davids for a crew change when returning to the South West with 6V53, the Etruria (Stoke-on-Trent) to St Blazey empty china clay hoods, on 15 March 1980. (Paul Townsend)

No. 50004 *St Vincent* runs alongside the estuary of the River Exe at Starcross on 14 March 1982. This is one of the sites where it is possible to see one of Brunel's original pumping stations for his abortive atmospheric railway. At this point on the journey, excitement would begin to build as the train approached the seawall. (Eddie Holden)

An undoubted highlight of a rail journey into Devon is the seawall stretch alongside the beach at Dawlish. Here Brunel's route threads through several short tunnels beneath the red sandstone headlands, such as here, at Coryton's Cove. No. 47411 disturbs the peace of the early morning beachgoers with the 23:45 Glasgow to Plymouth on 7 July 1987. (Lewis Bevan)

Crowds of holidaymakers on the beach seem oblivious to the temporary disturbance caused by No. 50045 *Achilles*, which is passing Dawlish station with 1V84, the 11:33 Manchester to Plymouth train, on 29 August 1983. The train would have featured electric haulage from Manchester via Crewe to Birmingham. (Stephen Dance)

Backed by the red sandstone cliffs of the English Riviera, No. 50034 *Furious* leans into the banked curve as she approaches Teignmouth with the 14:05 Bristol Temple Meads to Penzance on 8 July 1987. A couple of years earlier I got this same locomotive from Plymouth to St Erth at the start of my second term at Cornwall College. (Lewis Bevan)

The distinctive sound of the 2,700 hp English Electric power unit of No. 50018 *Resolution* will be amplified by the tall retaining wall at Teignmouth as she heads east on 8 May 1982. In a unique arrangement, the fifty Class 50s, or EE Type 4s as they were then known, began their life being leased from English Electric to BR. (Eddie Holden)

A Newcastle to Plymouth service headed by No. 45001 gets the thumbs up from a young enthusiast as dust is kicked up from the new ballast on the seawall at Teignmouth on 11 September 1978. The young girl in the photo possibly has children of her own now, but sadly they won't be waving at any Peaks if they holiday in Devon. (Syd Young)

No. 50038 *Formidable* storms along the seawall at Teignmouth with an Up train on 11 September 1978. These machines were despised by many Western Region enthusiasts when they were cascaded from the West Coast Main Line to replace the much-loved Western diesel-hydraulics. I still preferred the Class 50s to any Sulzer-engined locos though. (Syd Young)

The 14:25 Plymouth to Edinburgh service has a long way to go as it is viewed from Shaldon Bridge on the Teign Estuary. It is formed of a mixture of stock in three different liveries, which is hauled by Class 47 No. 47558 *Mayflower* on 5 July 1987. No. 47558 had previously been numbered D1599 and 47027. (Lewis Bevan)

Lit by the morning sun, 1C09, the 06:35 Bristol Temple Meads to Plymouth local train, is captured arriving at Newton Abbot's spacious station on 6 July 1984. Four of the vehicles are for parcels and newspaper traffic. The locomotive is No. 45139, which was built as D109 and entered service in 1961. She was withdrawn in 1987. (Dave Jolly)

One of the sights to look for at Newton Abbot was No. 24054, withdrawn in 1976 and renumbered as departmental No. TDB 968008. For many years she languished here among the Class 08 shunters and coaching stock. Happily, she is now preserved at Bury, where she is currently undergoing an overhaul. No. 50019 *Ramillies*, meanwhile, is drawing some stock from the sidings in this early 1980s view. (Eddie Holden)

No. 50010 *Monarch* passes Aller Junction on a short freight from the Plymouth direction on 7 May 1982. On the left, the branch for Torquay and Paignton diverges from the main line to Plymouth and Cornwall. The Class 50s were developed from the English Electric prototype DP2, which housed a 2,700 hp version of EE's sixteen-cylinder engine in a Deltic-style superstructure. (Eddie Holden)

No. 47512 arrives at the English Riviera resort of Paignton on 28 August 1982. Passengers can change here on to the Torbay & Dartmouth Railway for a steam train to Kingswear. This was a sad day for me, as 400 miles to the north I was travelling behind No. 40084 from Newcastle to York – the last time I would do so behind a Class 40 on the East Coast Main Line. (Syd Young)

Back on the main line to Cornwall, No. 50010 *Monarch* is in action again, drifting downhill past the sidings at Stoneycombe Quarry, just west of Aller Junction, on 18 April 1982. The signal is 'off' in the Down direction for a train, which will face the stiff climb to Dainton Summit, the first of the trio of South Devon banks, along with Rattery and Hemerdon. (Eddie Holden)

No. 45075 emerges from Dainton Tunnel and begins the descent towards Totnes with the 07:28 Leeds to Newquay train on 28 May 1983. The plywood signal box was a 1965 replacement for the old GWR structure. When the box became redundant in the late 1980s, it was moved to Westbury, where it is employed as the club room for the sailing club. (Nigel Hayman)

No. 50008 *Thunderer* works a lengthy mixed freight through Totnes, passing preserved GWR 0-6-0PT No. 1638 on a Dart Valley Railway train on 4 August 1987. Through running from the preserved branch line was short-lived because a BR crew was required to pilot each working into the BR station, which was an expensive business. On the right is the engine house that was built for Brunel's atmospheric railway. (Tim Saunders)

No. 47425 rolls into Totnes at the head of a SW–NE working on a sweltering 28 August 1982. An interesting assortment of cars, including a proper Mini can be seen on the Motorail flats, which are heading west for St Austell behind Class 50 No. 50007 *Hercules*. I remember watching with interest as my Dad drove his Ford Anglia on and off a similar train in the 1970s. (Syd Young)

The principal locomotive shed in the South West was Laira, on the eastern outskirts of Plymouth. It was one of the first purpose-built diesel traction maintenance depots in Britain when it opened in 1962, and it hosted an open day on 25 April 1982. No. 50023 *Howe* is on display outside the main building, alongside part of the re-railing train. (Colin Alexander)

The star attraction at that open day at Laira on 25 April 1982 was preserved Western Class 52 diesel-hydraulic No. D1023 *Western Fusilier*, from the National Collection at York. The last of the Westerns had been withdrawn only five years earlier, but No. D1023 is one of seven preserved out of the seventy-four built at Swindon and Crewe. (Ian Charles)

I was travelling from Newcastle to Plymouth on an HST on 1 May 1984; a power car had failed so No. 46028 was attached at Exeter to assist us over the Devon banks. The excitement was too much for the 46 though, and it caught fire just past Laira. Damage must have been slight as, once the fire brigade had finished, No. 46028 limped the last few hundred yards through Mutley Tunnel and into Plymouth. (Colin Alexander)

Double-heading was not uncommon, especially over the Devon banks, even if sometimes it was for operational reasons to save a 'path'. At a snowy Plymouth North Road, No. 50041 *Bulwark* and No. 50006 *Neptune* wait for departure time with the 08:53 Penzance to Newcastle train on 26 February 1986. (Carl Looker)

Western Region inspection saloon No. DB 999509 is hauled east through Plymouth North Road station by Class 50 No. 50039 *Implacable* in 1985. Meanwhile, the last of the Class, the former No. D449 No. 50049 *Defiance*, waits in the middle road. I liked the fact that the WR 'Warship' name tradition was resurrected when the Class 50s were named in the late 1970s. (Colin Alexander)

No. 50009 *Conqueror* is captured leaving Plymouth North Road with 1V85, the 09:22 Newcastle to Penzance train, on 11 July 1985. I had just completed the first of two terms at Plymouth Polytechnic as part of my course at Cornwall College, so I got to know the city quite well. (Dave Jolly)

Having just crossed the Tamar from Cornwall into Devon, No. 50037 *Illustrious* brings 1S86, the Penzance to Edinburgh train, off Brunel's 1859 Royal Albert Bridge on 30 August 1987. The main line is single track over the bridge. The scaffolding high above the Tamar is evidence of painting-work in progress and the 1960s road bridge towers alongside. (Mick Page)

One of many spectacular viaducts in Cornwall is this one at Liskeard, carrying the main line high above the branch line to Looe, which is seen in the foreground. An unidentified Class 45 or 46 heads a westbound ballast train on 13 September 1979. Like many Cornish viaducts, the upper part was initially constructed in timber. The rebuilt structure can be seen atop the original masonry piers. (Graham Roose)

264¾ miles from Paddington is Liskeard station. In this dramatically backlit telephoto shot, No. 45138 is bringing her train off the viaduct, seen on the opposite page, as she arrives with 1C11, the 07:50 Bristol Temple Meads to Penzance service, on 23 February 1985. (Dave Jolly)

No. 50046 *Ajax* arrives at Liskeard with 1V85, the 09:22 Newcastle to Penzance train, on 4 July 1984. Just above the locomotive the sharp curve leading to the Looe branch can be seen, passengers for which are well signposted to their connection at this most unusual junction station. (Dave Jolly)

Platform 3 at Liskeard is the point of departure for Looe branch trains and, unlike most junctions, it is at a right angle to the main line platforms. On 1 November 1986 this DMU set composed of No. W51305 and No. W51320 will set off north-east before taking a sharp horseshoe curve, descending to the valley bottom and reversing at Coombe Junction, where it will gain the branch proper. (Ian Charles)

The 10:35 Liskeard to Looe DMU is in the process of reversing at Coombe Junction on 10 June 1981. The line once continued beyond the station to quarries at Caradon, passing under Moorswater Viaduct, which can be seen beyond the train. This carries the main line west of Liskeard station. The base of the demolished signal box is in the foreground. (Kevin Weston)

St Pinnock Viaduct at Trago Mills is the location of one of the single-track sections of the main line. No. 50033 *Glorious* passes high above the valley with the 10:00 Penzance to Paddington on 22 August 1986. *Glorious* was taken into the National Railway Museum collection but was later disposed of. She is currently at the Birmingham Railway Museum, Tyseley. (Chris Holland)

Bodmin Parkway, named Bodmin Road until 1983, is the location for this fine study of No. 50008 *Thunderer* on 1S71, the 07:30 Penzance to Aberdeen train, on 30 June 1986. A few years later it became possible to change onto a steam train here once the preserved Bodmin and Wenford Railway opened. (Carl Looker)

The sinuous nature of Cornwall's main line is exaggerated by the telephoto lens as No. 50050 *Fearless* (formerly No. D400) approaches Bodmin Parkway on 2 July 1984. The train is 2C68, the 07:00 Exeter St Davids to Penzance stopping train. She is one of several Class 50s to survive in preservation. (Dave Jolly)

The next stop is Lostwithiel where No. 47415 is slowing for the station with 2C86, the 15:27 Penzance to Plymouth train, on 11 July 1985. The change in gradient and sharp curvature of the line are clearly visible in this shot. Lostwithiel is the junction for the Fowey branch, which carries china clay traffic. I love the company name on the lorry. (Dave Jolly)

Another Cornish junction is Par, for the Newquay branch, which is seen curving to the right here as No. 50033 *Glorious* arrives with an evening Penzance to Bristol Temple Meads train on 29 March 1988. Par is in the heart of china clay country. It looks like a train is about to set off along the branch, judging by the lower-quadrant home signal on the right. (Stephen McGahon)

When I arrived in Cornwall to start my college course, I was told it never snowed there. On this particular weekend, some of my Geordie mates, including the photographer, came to visit and brought the snow with them. No. 50041 *Bulwark* rounds the curve and slows into Par station with the 09:40 Paddington to Penzance service on 8 February 1986. I got No. 50046 *Ajax* from Camborne to Penzance on this day. (Ian Beattie)

By the mid-1980s, the plain corporate blue that had adorned everything was giving way to a variety of colour schemes. Railfreight-liveried and snowplough-fitted No. 37196 *Tre, Pol and Pen* arrives light engine from the Newquay direction at Par on 8 February 1986. She has almost certainly travelled the short distance from St Blazey shed, which is around the tight curve. (Ian Beattie)

BR Sulzer Class 25 No. 25223 has arrived at Par with a rake of china clay 'hoods' from Burngullow on 12 June 1980. The locomotive has run-round the train, which will now be propelled out of the station towards Lostwithiel before being hauled onto the Newquay branch to St Blazey. (Kevin Weston)

Of the Cornish branch lines that survived into the 1980s, Newquay was by far the busiest, and the only one boasting regular main line trains. No. 50006 *Neptune* waits at the coastal terminus for departure with 1E65, the 09:18 to Newcastle, on 5 July 1986. The station has since been reduced to a single platform. (Dave Jolly)

Further west on the main line, St Austell was the Motorail terminal for Cornwall, with dedicated sidings for the loading and unloading of cars whose occupants had travelled in the comfort of the coaching stock. Those days were long gone by the time No. 50038 *Formidable* arrived here with 1E91, the 08:53 Penzance to Newcastle, on 23 February 1985. (Dave Jolly)

The former Motorail sidings where Dad's Ford Anglia was unloaded in 1973, top right, are redundant by the time Class 50 pairing No. 50027 *Lion* and No. 50032 *Courageous* wait at St Austell on 3 June 1981. The train is the 13:45 Penzance to Paddington, a service that regularly produced a pair of 50s through Cornwall. (Eddie Holden)

The county town of Cornwall is Truro, and its station is the junction for Falmouth branch trains. No. 50027 *Lion* calls here with 1V85, the 09:22 Newcastle to Penzance train, on 2 July 1984. The formation is typical of the time, with air-conditioned Mk 2 coaches augmented by a Mk 1 full brake at the front and a Mk 1 catering vehicle sixth. (Dave Jolly)

Three coaches is hardly a taxing load for a filthy No. 50012 *Benbow* as she leaves Truro on 1 November 1986 with what is probably a Plymouth to Penzance train. The long footbridge provided an excellent vantage point for photographers and trainspotters. (Ian Charles)

In contrast to No. 50012 above, sister No. 50024 *Vanguard* looks smart in Network SouthEast livery at the east end of Truro station on 16 July 1988. Yet another destination served by trains from the South West was Milton Keynes, and this was the 15:02 from Penzance to the Buckinghamshire new town. (Carl Looker)

The Falmouth branch was mostly DMU-operated, but for a four-year period in the late 1970s and early '80s there was a through train to Paddington at 09:10. This was formed by the stock from the 08:22 Truro to Falmouth 'stopper'. For one year there was also a Paddington to Falmouth train arriving around 17:00. No. 50018 *Resolution* is seen here at the branch terminus on 4 August 1979. (Brian Aston)

Summer services could bring rarities such as No. 47380, lacking any kind of train heating at all. This is Redruth in the heart of tin-mining country, and the train is 2C74 – the '2' denoting a stopping passenger train. In this case it is the 16:35 Plymouth to Penzance on 2 July 1984. Redruth's Methodist Church is the large building on the left. (Dave Jolly)

A different view of Redruth station from the footbridge. Class 50 No. 50025 *Invincible* is about to disappear under Fore Street as she heads for Plymouth in 1985. The Class 50s had been the mainstay of accelerated West Coast Main Line trains from Crewe to Glasgow, often working in pairs. On completion of the WCML electrification, they were reallocated to the Western Region. (Colin Alexander)

At Carn Brea, the ex-GWR main line between Camborne and Redruth passes through a variety of industrial landscapes, with relics of tin mining interspersed with modern commercial units. With the buildings of my old college in the background, No. 50016 *Barham* heads towards Redruth and Plymouth in 1986. (Colin Alexander)

No. 45048 *The Royal Marines* calls at Camborne with the relief working to the 10:20 Penzance to Newcastle on 29 December 1983. The road up the hill to the left of this level crossing was where Richard Trevithick carried out one of his early steam engine experiments, remembered in the song 'Going Up Camborne Hill Coming Down'. (Graham Wise/Kevin Lane collection)

The driver of Class 50 No. 50012 *Benbow* opens her throttle as she approaches Hayle station in Cornwall with an Up parcels train on 4 September 1979. At this time Hayle boasted a freight-only branch line, which is seen curving downhill steeply to the right of the picture, to the wharves. This featured what is thought to be the world's first sand drag. The branch closed in 1982. (Syd Young)

St Erth is the last stop before Penzance and is the junction for the St Ives branch. When I lived in St Ives and travelled to college in Camborne, I would sometimes commute by train. No. 50007 *Sir Edward Elgar* leaves with an Up postal in 1984. St Erth used to handle significant milk traffic for London. (Colin Alexander)

The St Ives branch is a jewel in Cornwall's railway crown, revealing stunning coastal views such as this at Carbis Bay, the penultimate stop on the 4¼-mile line, which is seen here on 3 July 1983. In its glory days, GWR Prairie tanks would bustle along the branch with through 'Cornish Riviera Express' coaches from Paddington. By the 1980s, three-car DMUs were the order of the day and in the off season, a single car sufficed. (Geoff Brown)

No. 47629 passes the site of the former Marazion station, having just left Penzance with the 11:04 service to Glasgow Central/Edinburgh Waverley on Sunday, 29 January 1989. The former Pullman cars in the old goods yard on the left were used for many years as camping coaches and later for staff holidays. At least two survive as part of a hotel in Petworth. (Nigel Tregoning)

On the home straight now, and one of Penzance's 350 hp Class 08 shunters brings the vans of the Paddington postal train from the sidings at Long Rock towards Penzance station on 11 September 1985. The view from the train at this point is a magnificent sweeping panorama of Mounts Bay and St Michael's Mount. (Geoff Brown)

It's the end of the line, and we have travelled 657 miles from Edinburgh. From Penzance, it's a bus ride to Land's End or the *Scillonian* ferry to the beautiful Scilly Isles. If you prefer you could jump on 1S87, the 10:30 to Glasgow Central, seen with the 5,400 hp combination of No. 50029 *Renown* and No. 50027 *Lion* on 27 June 1987. (Dave Jolly)

The buffer stops at Penzance are just over 300 miles from Paddington, and are as far west as you can go by train in England. No. 50007 *Hercules* waits for her empty stock to be shunted on 25 April 1982. Two HSTs are alongside on Paddington services. Today's Voyagers do the journey from Penzance to Edinburgh in the time it used to take to reach Newcastle, but I would rather be back in the early '80s. (Ian Charles)